What I Thought I Knew and What I Know Now

What I Thought I Knew and What I Know Now

Antonio Banks

Published by Antonio Banks, 2024.

WHAT I THOUGHT I KNEW AND WHAT I KNOW NOW

First edition. October 1, 2024.

ISBN: 979-8227366108

Written by Antonio Banks.

To my beloved mother,Whose strength and wisdom shaped my understanding of love and resilience. Your unwavering spirit continues to guide me in all that I do.

To my children,May you find inspiration in my journey and forge your paths with courage and integrity. You are my greatest treasures, and I hope to equip you for life's challenges.

And to everyone who has felt lost or misunderstood,This book is for you. May it remind you that your story matters and that there is always hope for growth and redemption.

Dedication

To my beloved mother,
Whose strength and wisdom shaped my understanding of love and resilience. Your unwavering spirit continues to guide me in all that I do.
To my children,
May you find inspiration in my journey and forge your paths with courage and integrity. You are my greatest treasures, and I hope to equip you for life's challenges.
And to everyone who has felt lost or misunderstood,
This book is for you. May it remind you that your story matters and that there is always hope for growth and redemption.

Introduction

My name is Antonio Banks, #00591869. Let me tell you about the significance of the number that comes after my name, as it will remain an everlasting part of my identity later in this book. I was born on October 4, 1985, at 8:41 a.m. to Mary (22) and Herman Banks (37) in George W. Hubbard Hospital in Nashville, Tennessee. What can I say? Mom loved older guys. Despite my father's imperfections and flaws, his absence profoundly affected me.

Chapter 1

Growing up without a father figure left a deep and lasting void in my life—one that I still grapple with today. My firm and determined mother took on the immense responsibility of raising my brother and me independently. She did her best to fill the gaps, but the absence of a father was always palpable. We missed learning the essential lessons fathers often impart to their sons: how to be men, respect women, and be good fathers. Even the simpler things, like tossing a football, playing basketball, or going fishing, were experiences we longed for but never had.

As children, my brother and I were naturally curious about why our father was no longer around. When we asked, my mother would tell us stories about his absence. It wasn't easy for her to share, but she wanted us to understand. She told us that one of the reasons they separated was because of his gambling problem. It was so severe that he would steal the money she had painstakingly saved for rent and groceries. That betrayal cut deep, knowing that the man supposed to provide for and protect us was instead contributing to our hardship. The second reason was his drinking. It wasn't just beer he was consuming—it was whiskey and a lot of it. His drinking was so excessive that he often wouldn't come home until three or four in the morning. My mother, still young and hopeful, would sometimes go out with him, thinking that sharing what he enjoyed might bring them closer and save their marriage. But it only made things worse. My father was a ladies' man, and my mother's presence cramped his style. It wasn't long before he asked one of his so-called friends to walk her home, supposedly to keep her safe. But that night, he turned into a nightmare. The man my father trusted tried to assault my mother, and if it hadn't been for the timely intervention of a neighbor, he might have succeeded. My mother always said it was a blessing that someone came to her aid just in time.

When my father finally got home and learned what had happened, he was furious. He confronted the man, but it didn't end well for him. One of the man's friends crept up behind my father and struck him on the head with a two-by-four that had a nail sticking out of it. The blow knocked him unconscious. The men dragged him to his car, and one of them, after driving around the block several times, told my mother she might want to take him to the hospital before he died. She found him in the backseat, lying in a pool of blood—it was so much that she said it looked like someone had gutted a hog. In a panic, she drove as fast as she could to the hospital. They rushed him into surgery, and although he survived, the doctors told her that if she had been even three minutes later, he wouldn't have made it. Another blessing, she called it.

The final reason for their divorce, my mother told us, was the other women. He had been unfaithful, and the women he was involved with took pleasure in tormenting my mother, flaunting their affairs and rubbing her pain in her face. But my mother wasn't one to be pushed around—not by my father or anyone. She stood up for herself, fiercely protecting her dignity and her beliefs. Looking back, I see how much strength and courage it took for her to navigate those years and raise us boys in the face of adversity. She was, without a doubt, a true warrior—a savage, as some might say, in the best possible way.

Her resilience and unwavering strength have shaped who I am today. Even though I still feel the void left by my father's absence, I know that the lessons my mother taught me through her actions and words are invaluable. She showed me that no matter how difficult life gets, we have the power to rise above our circumstances and stand tall. She was, and always will be, my greatest inspiration.

.

Chapter 2

Living in a single-parent household tested my mom's resilience and perseverance like nothing else. The challenges she faced were immense, and the sacrifices she made were countless. Yet, she kept us through it all, even when it seemed impossible.

My mom worked two jobs to make ends meet, but even then, money was tight. Daycare was out of the question, so she found a more affordable option with an in-home babysitter. Despite her tireless efforts, she was constantly forced to make difficult decisions about what bills to pay and which necessities we could afford.

Ultimately, she decided to live without electricity for months to save enough money to keep us fed and clothed. Our home, already cramped and modest, became even more challenging. Candles replaced our lights, a cooler became our refrigerator, and we relied on kerosene heaters for warmth. The smell of kerosene is one I'll never forget; it lingers in my memory as a constant reminder of those hard times. We lived in a small, one-bedroom home, all sharing a single sleeping space and bathroom. Without electricity, even the simplest tasks became monumental challenges. My brother and I were typical kids, always playing outside and coming in covered in dirt and grass stains.

My mom had to get creative without hot water, which required electricity. She boiled water on the stove, carefully mixing it with cold water in the bathtub so it wouldn't burn us. She bathed us together to conserve water and time, but for herself, she boiled a separate pot of water—one small luxury in a life where luxuries were few and far between.

Laundry was another struggle. With no washer or dryer, my mom washed our clothes in the bathtub and hung them outside on a clothesline to dry. When it rained, the clothes got soaked and often smelled sour, making us easy targets for teasing and ridicule. It wasn't very respectful, but there was nothing we could do. My mom was doing everything she could, and that was enough for us.

Despite all of this, my mom never showed weakness. Not once did she let us see the weight of her struggles. I'm sure there were countless nights when she wanted to collapse in exhaustion or break down in tears, but she never did—at least not in front of us. She kept going, kept fighting, kept figuring it out. She never asked for help from the government, friends, or even our dad. She didn't want to owe anyone anything or be reminded of favors granted. Her pride and determination were unwavering.

On some nights, when handwashing clothes was too much, she would gather all our dirty laundry and take us to the laundromat. She'd go late at night when it was quiet, and there was no wait for the machines. It took hours to wash and dry everything, so long that my brother and I would eventually fall asleep on the warm, freshly folded clothes. When it was finally time to go home, she'd gently wake us, and we'd make the long walk back. The feeling of being tucked into bed after those nights is something I'll always cherish—a reminder that no matter how tough things were, we were safe, loved, and together. My mom's strength, refusal to give up, and ability to make something out of nothing taught me the true meaning of resilience. She showed me there's always a way forward, even in the darkest times. Her sacrifices and unwavering determination have shaped who I am today. I owe everything to her and the incredible example she set.

Chapter 3

As my brother and I grew older, we noticed more of the realities around us. We started to understand our hardships and the resilience it took for our mom to keep us going. One thing that became increasingly clear was how often we moved. I don't think we stayed in one place for over a year. Whenever we settled in, made new friends, and got used to our surroundings, it was time to pack up and move again. It was frustrating. But one move stood out because it brought us closer to our dad.

This was a challenging yet significant change. Despite all the pain and betrayal my mom had endured because of my dad, she found the courage to involve him in our lives. It wasn't easy for her, but she did it because she knew it was the right thing to do for us. And in many ways, it proved beneficial, even for her. With Dad nearby, she no longer had to worry about paying a babysitter. Dad, who was on disability after his earlier accident, had time to look after us and sometimes worked a few hours at a Texaco gas station to keep busy.

I remember spending time at that Texaco station when Mom had errands to run. Those visits were some of the most fun times we had with Dad. We could eat as much candy as we wanted and drink as many Slush Puppies as possible. If you're unfamiliar with a Slush Puppy, let me explain: it's a non-carbonated frozen drink with tiny ice pellets and flavored syrup. Back then, there were four primary flavors: Raspberry, Cherry, Lime, and Strawberry. We'd mix and match the flavors, creating our sugary concoctions. Slush Puppies still exist, but there are probably more flavors now than in the '90s.

Mom wasn't thrilled when she picked us up after these sugar-filled visits. We either complained about stomachaches or bounced off the walls, making her life more challenging. She wasn't happy with Dad for letting us indulge so much, but it never really changed his ways.

Living closer to Dad meant that Mom had to commute further to her job. She started looking for something closer, and it didn't take long before she found a job at the Tennessee Mat Company. I don't think the company exists anymore, but it was an excellent opportunity for her back then. The job was better than her previous ones, and even though we still struggled financially, it wasn't as bad as it had been.

When summer came around, and school was out, it took a lot of pressure off Mom. My brother and I would spend most of the summer with Dad, which we didn't mind. The tricky part was getting back to Mom. Although she and Dad could tolerate each other, they weren't particularly invested in coordinating our drop-offs and pick-ups. So, we had to ride the city bus from Dad's house to Mom's work.

That bus ride was terrifying for us as kids. Nashville's city buses back then were nothing like they are today. They were a refuge for many homeless people who stayed on board to escape the heat. Some people didn't even get off to use the restroom, which meant the bus often smelled of urine and feces. We saw people doing drugs, overdosing, and sometimes even pulling out guns in moments of desperation or panic. Being alone on a bus surrounded by these dangers was incredibly scary as a child. We never knew if we'd make it to our destination safely. But when we did, it was always a huge relief.

When we finally arrived at Mom's workplace, they would put my brother and me in the break room until her shift ended. We'd spend that time doing homework or playing, and some of her coworkers would check on us occasionally, sometimes even bringing us snacks. One man in particular, Curtis, stood out. My mom always said God sent him into our lives—not romantically, but as friends. Curtis was kind and generous, taking us under his wing without hesitation. He helped us in ways he didn't have to, without expecting anything in return.

Curtis was indeed a gift from God. He brought a sense of stability and support when we needed it most. His kindness and selflessness left a lasting impact on our lives, and even though he's no longer with us, I'll always remember how he quietly made our lives a little bit easier. My mom was right—he was a blessing, and we were fortunate to have known him.

Those years were filled with challenges, uncertainty, and moments of love, resilience, and unexpected kindness. Despite all he had done, my mom's courage to involve our dad and the support we received from people like Curtis taught me valuable lessons about forgiveness, strength, and the importance of helping others whenever possible.

Chapter 4

Life in the projects brought a harsh reality we had to confront daily. Moving in with my aunt down south marked a new chapter filled with unexpected challenges and moments of growth. Despite everything she had endured, my mother forgave her sister for past betrayals and took the risk of living with her again. Forgiveness is a powerful force; my mother embodied that, even when it meant putting herself in a vulnerable position for our sake.

The projects were not just a place to live but a battlefield. The constant threat of violence was part of our daily lives. Every time we stepped outside, we navigated a minefield of broken glass, used needles, and the remnants of the previous night's violence. Gunshots were a nightly occurrence, a grim reminder that we were living in a war zone. We learned to take cover at the sound of gunfire, hiding behind block walls until the chaos subsided.

But even in this environment, there were small pockets of joy. My aunt's daughter, our cousin, had a playroom filled with dolls and toys that were off-limits to us. We sometimes played with her—not out of interest in the dolls, but from a desire to protect her from the loneliness we knew too well. Tragically, her life was cut short at thirteen due to diabetes, a loss that still lingers in our memories.

We found refuge next door at our grandmother's house, where her adopted children introduced us to the world of video games. The Sega Genesis became our escape from the harsh realities outside. Yet, even here, darkness found us. Those we should have been able to trust took advantage of our innocence, bribing us with access to their games and toys, coercing us into silence and submission. The fear of losing our place to stay kept us quiet, trapping us in a cycle of abuse that we didn't know how to break.

Sports became our salvation. Football and basketball offered us a way out, a means to channel our pain into something positive. We threw ourselves into these games, not just for the joy they brought us, but because they gave us a purpose—a way to rise above the circumstances that tried to hold us down. My mother supported us wholeheartedly, becoming a cheerleading coach and a football mom, finding her sense of purpose in our achievements. Through these activities, she met the man who would become her husband, a football coach and truck driver who brought a new sense of stability to our lives.

However, with this new relationship came a painful reality. When he stayed over, my brother and I would go next door to our grandmother's house, where the abuse continued. We found ourselves trapped in a terrible situation, torn between the need for a safe place to live and the horrors we faced there. Speaking out seemed impossible; the fear of being homeless kept us silent.

Looking back, I realize that our strength wasn't just surviving those times but finding ways to rise above them. We learned to forgive, endure, and find hope in the darkest circumstances. We drew strength from each other, and the small moments of joy kept us going. My mother remained our rock; her resilience and determination have shaped who I am today.

Our journey was far from easy, but it taught us the value of perseverance, the importance of family, and the power of forgiveness. It's a testament to the human spirit's ability to endure, to find light even in the darkest places, and to keep moving forward, no matter what.

Chapter 5

Then came the day we moved again, but this time, it felt different. There was a sense of relief that things might change for the better. We were leaving behind the challenges, the danger, and the familiar streets of Nashville. Our new destination was Mount Juliet, Tennessee—a small town that promised a fresh start. My mother's boyfriend, whose family lived there, prompted the move. It starkly contrasted with the big city life we were accustomed to, and the unfamiliarity was daunting. None of us knew anyone, not even his family, and stepping into the unknown was scary.

Despite the anxiety of starting over, my mother, in her usual resilient way, quickly found a job working as a janitor at my school. I'll never forget my first day at that school. I was met with so many strange looks that I felt as if I were some oddity. It wasn't because of anything I said or did, but simply because I stood out—at six feet tall, I towered over the other elementary school kids. My height didn't go unnoticed for long; basketball and football coaches soon approached me, eager to have me try out once I hit middle school. I embraced both sports with all my passion. Sports had always been my escape, a way to channel my energy and find a sense of belonging, and that continued here in Mount Juliet.

But just as things seemed to be falling into place, life threw me a curveball. During my first year in high school, I broke my leg in two places while playing football. It was a devastating injury that not only ended my sports career but also crushed my spirit. With sports no longer an option, I lost my sense of direction and purpose. As if life wasn't complicated enough, I became a father for the first time at seventeen. I had two children by eighteen while still trying to finish high school. The weight of responsibility was too much, and I felt lost without the outlet of sports. I convinced myself there was no point in staying in school if I couldn't play, so I dropped out during my junior year.

Dropping out wasn't the start of a new chapter; it was the beginning of a downward spiral. Instead of stepping up to the responsibilities of fatherhood, I chose to do what I wanted. I let my children's mothers bear the brunt of raising them while I continued to make poor choices. My third child was born not long after by a different woman, and even then, I didn't change. I got a job when my daughter was born, but my immaturity and irresponsibility led to my being fired within a few months. Once again, my mother had to step in, taking care of my kids just as she had taken care of me.

It's a painful truth, but I was okay with it. I was OK with not being the father my children needed because, in my twisted logic, I was following in the footsteps of my father. I had always looked up to him, believing he was supposed to be my mentor and role model. But I followed him down the wrong path, becoming the kind of father he was—absent, unreliable, and selfish.

For years, I was a father in name only. I would see my kids when it was convenient for me when I didn't have other plans. Weeks would go by without me visiting them, sometimes even months. I missed countless birthdays, football games, and cheerleading competitions. I made promises I never intended to keep. It's heartbreaking to acknowledge, but that was the reality. I transitioned from being a dad—a loving, attentive caregiver—to just a father, someone who was biologically connected to his children but emotionally distant and disconnected. I lived with my mother and stepfather until I was 24, going through the motions of life but never truly living. I went to church every Sunday, hoping to find guidance, but I never really sought the help I needed to become a better man, a better dad. I was too wrapped up in trying to control my life, too stubborn to ask for help. I wanted to live on my terms, not realizing that I was throwing away the most precious things in my life—my children, my future, and my sense of self-worth. Looking back, I see how my journey, as painful and misguided as it was, has shaped who I am today. I've learned that being a father isn't just about bringing children into the world; it's about being there for them, guiding them, and ensuring they know they are loved and valued. It's about stepping up, even when it's hard, and putting their needs above your own. My past is filled with regrets and lessons that I hope to pass on to others so they don't make the same mistakes I did. I've realized that life isn't about living on your terms; it's about living a life worthy of the love and trust of those who depend on you. It's about redemption, growth, and the strength to become the person you were always meant to be. While I can't change the past, I can work daily to be the man, the father, and the role model my children deserve. It's a long road, but I'm committed to walking it, no matter how difficult it may be.

Chapter 6

At age 20, I finally found a job I would stick with for a little longer than usual. I met a woman I liked, and one day, when I was supposed to be off, I received a text from her—her actual number—asking if I could help her for a couple of hours. Of course, I said yes. This was my chance to win her over. It took work, but we started dating after many texts and a little consistency.

She had another child from a previous relationship, but like me, his dad wasn't around either. I often wondered how I could help care for another man's kid when I couldn't even care for myself. Still, I was willing to try. I was ready to put more effort into helping her care for her child than caring for my own. The motivation was clear: I wanted to leave my mother's house, and she had her apartment.

Did I genuinely care for her then, or was she just my means of escape? I was desperate to get away from my mother's house because I could not stand my stepdad. He drank from Monday through Sunday, and while we went to church on Sunday mornings, by evening, he was already drunk. His drinking had stained his eyes yellow over the years. He attempted to be abusive, but it never ended well for him; my mother wasn't going to endure that again. She had dealt with it with my father and wasn't about to go through it again.

A year into our relationship, we moved in together in a duplex in Mount Juliet, closer to her work since she was a manager. But once again, I found myself without a job. And then came the news: "I am expecting my fourth child." I was excited, just as I had been for my other three children, but was I ready? Not at all.

I was unprepared for another child. I couldn't keep a steady job, couldn't afford to help her pay the bills, and certainly wasn't mature enough for another baby. Because I couldn't provide for them, we faced yet another move. She saw that I wasn't ready for this responsibility. On my twenty-first birthday, she made the painful decision to have an abortion. It was heartbreaking. We tried to work through the aftermath, but I harbored so much resentment that it was difficult for me to accept and move on.

Eventually, we drifted apart while still sleeping together, leading to another unexpected pregnancy. This time, she decided to keep the baby, bringing us back together—what a complicated love story. On September 23, 2009, my fourth child was born.

Chapter 7

I finally settled down and asked her to marry me, and to my relief, she said yes. On October 10, 2010, we tied the knot. I was finally going to be in one of my children's lives—there for every birthday, his first crawl, and his first steps. I was excited at the prospect of watching him grow up. I secured a decent job and even got my vehicle. Things seemed to be looking up for me.

But looking back, I can see things were looking up for me, not my family. I was selfish and greedy. I wanted what I wanted instead of being responsible. I would rather spend seventy dollars on a game when the rent was due. If my truck payment was due, I chose to spend money on steroids and protein shakes. We needed groceries, but I would buy a new gaming headset instead. Yes, that was how greedy and selfish I was. I prioritized my habits over taking care of my family. I left all the responsibilities to her.

What a great husband I was—sarcasm intended. I was a husband mooching off my wife, knowing she would pick up the slack if I didn't. It became a habit. I lost my two-year job, and my truck got repossessed. Suddenly, I had to rely on her to take me places or walk wherever needed. My selfishness led to us moving again, this time in with her mother in a two-bedroom trailer with twin bunk beds. Her son slept on the top bunk because he was the oldest, while my wife, son, and I squeezed into the bottom bunk. It was a tight fit, but that's how we lived because I was an irresponsible husband and father.

I put my family in situations that could have been easily avoided. Instead of fixing the problems, I made them worse. I made excuses rather than taking responsibility for my actions. I would find minor issues and blow them out of proportion, using them as excuses to have affairs. This led to more lies, arguments, and fights. Why couldn't I figure it out? Because I didn't want to, and I liked having two women. I knew the other one wouldn't if my wife said no.

My mother always told me, "You are your father's child." I denied it, but I was just like him. The only traits I didn't inherit from my dad were his gambling and drinking habits. I was content with my secret relationships, unfaithfulness, and my dependence not just on my spouse but on others. Did I want to be different? Of course, it felt too good in my mind and body, especially when I thought I could get away with it. It became an addiction. My sins and wickedness consumed my life.

I tried to change. I even attended a nearby church that claimed to follow God. I loved the pastor; I thought he was teaching the proper principles of the Bible, even though I never saw an actual Bible on the pews. He never picked one up to read from it, and I was convinced he was so knowledgeable that he didn't need one. I believed this was the true Gospel, so I decided to get baptized. Although I didn't know much about it, I understood that being submerged symbolized the death of my old self and that I would be reborn in Christ. But that wasn't the case for me; the old me stayed. I tried to convince others that I was new, pretending to be something I wasn't on the outside, but deep down, I knew I hadn't changed.

Nobody knew my truth, or so I thought. But she knew all along what I was doing. For some reason, she never left. She kept hoping—and I'm sure praying—that one day I would change.

Chapter 8

23

In 2013, she bought our first-ever house, and I had been cheating for years. Why? Why did she continue to do things she could have stopped long ago? Most of you reading this probably think you would have divorced me by now, and I can't blame you for feeling that way—she should have, too. But for some odd reason, she kept holding on. So, I kept cheating, and I kept lying. Despite having what most people would love to have, I took it all for granted.

Because of my wrongdoing, the woman I had been having an affair with ended up pregnant. When she found out, it was the last straw for my wife. We grew apart; she would go out and not come home until the next day. I slept in a different room, and sometimes she would even kick me out because, technically, it was her house. I would leave but return when things calmed down or seemed to settle.

Then, one morning, I received a phone call from the woman I had gotten pregnant, only to learn that she had miscarried four months into her pregnancy. Even though it was wrong, it still hurt. My mom always used to say that things happen for a reason, and perhaps she was right. My mom asked if she could move in with us a few months later. I agreed though I knew it would cause more tension; I didn't care that she was my mother. She moved in because the people she worked for and attended church had done something unexpected. They banded together with a few members of her church to buy a house that needed work, but to Mom, it felt like gold. A year later, she moved into her new home.

The real question was this: Why could I never figure life out? Why was it so difficult for me to step up and be a man? Why did I always feel the need to have multiple partners? Did I have an addiction? I couldn't figure life out because I thought I didn't have to; everything was handed to me. I got it whenever I asked for something because I was the youngest. My lack of a father figure or role model left me without the tools to learn how to be a man or a father.

I felt the need to have multiple partners because I always saw my dad with different women, and I thought that was normal. I could have easily broken that cycle, but I chose not to. My mom, who had gone through the same experiences as my dad, even tried to coach me and tell me what I was doing was wrong. She invited me to the church she attended, but I refused her invitation. Why? Because I felt that I didn't need anyone trying to change me; I wanted to be myself. Still, she persisted every Sunday, promising I wouldn't be the same when I walked out of that place. Of course, I was skeptical.

Eventually, I reluctantly went. As a son, you learn that when your mom tells you something, nine times out of ten, she's right—and she was. I fell in love with that church, and soon, we all did. It became our routine. Things were looking up. I became a church member, got involved, and started reading and studying the Bible and Christian books. It felt good to change.

Then, one day, I received a call from a detective asking if I had time to talk. I assumed they wanted to discuss a recent incident involving a friend of mine who had overdosed. I said yes, and after that, my life changed drastically.

Chapter 9

On December 17, 2015, I was arrested and charged with a sex offense, which forever labeled me a sex offender and placed me on the registry for life.

Before you hastily dismiss this book due to my charge, let me clarify being a sex offender does not equate to being a pedophile or a child molester. It does NOT mean one is automatically guilty. This label does not define who I truly am.

After my arrest, I posted bond and moved in with my mom in Lebanon, Tennessee. I yearned to continue growing in my faith at a church that wouldn't alter my identity. Unfortunately, the church I chose did change me. I was determined to keep moving forward, believing nothing could hinder my progress. But then, everything changed.

I got out on a Friday and attended church on Sunday, only to receive a message on Facebook suggesting that I should not return until my legal matters were resolved. You can imagine the heartbreak I felt.

Ultimately defeated, I considered surrendering to despair. But something within me urged me not to give in. Instead, I confronted the hypocrisy I observed—the church's teachings that were not being practiced. Matthew 9:12 states, "Those who are well do not need a physician, but those who are sick." That was the message they preached. My mistake was relying on man instead of God.

I fought tirelessly until 2018 when I was sentenced to five years in prison with the possibility of parole after one year. During this time, I received my inmate ID number, which I had to write out every time I sent a letter, saw the nurse, or used the phone. Hearing my mom hit the ground, crying out in anguish, was a harrowing experience. Yet, we were determined to face the challenges ahead with unwavering confidence, believing we would emerge from this situation more vital than ever.

Though we prayed for a different outcome, I chose to use this time as an opportunity for growth. I asked my mom to send me my Bible, and once it arrived—after about a week—I gathered a few inmates and proposed starting a Bible study group. They agreed, and we met every day. I also wrote to specific churches requesting Bible studies, which further nourished my faith.

About a month into my sentence, a pastor came to preach at the jail. He reminded me of the pastor I used to listen to before my arrest, able to recite Bible verses from memory without opening the book. Though I can't recall his sermon's specific topic, it profoundly impacted me. After experiencing the transformative power of my first baptism, I decided to be baptized again. This time, I felt as if my old self had died, and I emerged from the water renewed. I truly felt different. I even wrote to the church I had been attending, asking for forgiveness for my past behavior. I didn't expect a response, which was fine; I intended to do what was right in God's eyes.

I remained in county jail until my parole hearing in 2019. Unfortunately, the hearing did not go as I had hoped, and I accepted the outcome as it was meant to be. Parole informed me that I would have to serve the remaining four years of my sentence. It hurt deeply, but I clung to my faith even more fiercely.

During my time in jail, I witnessed many things, including what I call "jailhouse religion" at its finest. I'm not suggesting that people in prison don't change because I did. Still, I learned that when someone first enters jail and speaks passionately about their faith, it can be disheartening to see them back in court for the exact charges within a month of their release or to see them no longer holding a Bible or speaking about Jesus.

My baptism this time was a commitment to remain faithful to God and to continue on the path of righteousness, regardless of the outcomes that lay ahead.

Chapter 10

29

What I thought I knew was that I could control everything. But what I know now is that this belief was false. It's easy to think we ultimately control our lives and the world around us, but the truth is that some things are beyond our control. I eventually found myself out of control of my own life.

In prison, I had to adhere to a strict schedule for everything—designated bedtimes, specific shower times, limits on phone usage, and even time restrictions on meals. After being denied parole, the county jail sent me to prison, where I could only bring a Bible, a few phone numbers, and a couple of pictures. The rest of my belongings would have to be stored as property, and my mom would need to pick them up.

Then, we were placed in the back of what I call an "animal control van," handcuffed and shackled. They informed us it would take two hours to reach the prison. I was extremely nervous, often hearing negative stories about prisons, and with my charge, people would tell me I wouldn't make it.

When I arrived at the prison at eight o'clock, it took another two hours to reach where I was supposed to be. I had to adjust to a vastly different prison life. I remember a week into my stay when a guy thought another inmate had used his PIN to make a phone call. In a fit of rage, he stabbed the other man in the eye with a pencil. It was a horrifying sight, but it didn't change who I am now. I remained true to myself, with no intention of pretending to be someone I was not. I continued my Bible studies and started a prayer group with other inmates, which we held every night. After two weeks, I moved to a different unit—one that was significantly better, known as the work pod. This meant we had privileges that many others didn't. We could work, watch TV, use the phone all day, and play softball, frisbee, chess, or basketball. As strange as it sounds, it was excellent; it made time faster.

I also began taking college courses in seminary and theology through the mail. Although I had to pay for it, they only took a percentage since we only earned sixteen cents an hour. It was a fantastic program. Although I could no longer control anything, I believed God could. I surrendered everything to Him and trusted Him completely, which was my best decision ever. While this surrender was empowering, my life was still far from easy. It didn't make things simpler or prevent bad days filled with loneliness, depression, frustration, or anger. I had my share of those days, often experiencing more bad than good ones. However, it was about how I dealt with them. Did I resolve them independently? Absolutely.

"Knowing that God is in control and trusting Him to empower us to overcome our weaknesses is the ultimate source of strength and inspiration."

Chapter 11

After eight months in prison, I received a write-up and a disciplinary report for violating prison rules. The incident occurred when outside personnel took my Bible from me, citing that no reading material or personal belongings could be brought from our cells to work. Despite this, I decided to get my Bible and homework, as we often had long stretches of downtime during work, serving meals to other inmates and then waiting two hours for dinner.

Unfortunately, my decision didn't end well. During a search after my shift, they found my Bible, confiscating it once again. Afterward, I repeatedly asked for it to be returned, but weeks passed without a response. Frustrated and desperate to retrieve my most treasured possession—my relationship with God—I filled out the proper paperwork, but still, there was no answer. I even asked my mother to call the prison, but nothing changed.

2 Peter 3:15 states, "Always be ready to give a defense of the faith that is in you." I was ready, even if it meant facing consequences I despised. Eventually, my actions landed me in solitary confinement, a place reserved for serious disciplinary issues like violence or attempts to escape.

In the hole, I was locked down for twenty-three hours a day and allowed only an hour for phone calls and showers. My only possessions were hygiene items, and I ate twice a day—often cold food. It was a tough situation, but the struggle was worth it. After some time, a correctional officer finally returned my Bible to me. I felt immense gratitude for having it back; it gave me comfort and guidance daily. Two weeks back, I was told to pack again in my previous work unit.

This time, however, I was moving to a unit with fewer privileges, returning to lockdown, and having to wait for gang members to finish their calls before I could contact my loved ones. The phone situation was frustrating, and sometimes, I couldn't even reach out to anyone because of our limited time.

Yes, I had options, but the alternatives could have led to dangerous situations or extended my time behind bars. Proverbs 3:5- 6 reminds us to "Trust in the Lord with all your heart and lean not on your understanding. In all your ways acknowledge Him, and He will direct your paths." Relying solely on my knowledge often led me into difficult situations.

I spent a month in the new unit before being told to pack up again. This move felt different, though; my mother had prayed fervently that it wouldn't happen. So, why did God allow it? Romans 8:18 reassures us: "I consider that our present sufferings are not worth comparing with the glory that will be revealed in us."

Chapter 12

On September 20, 2020, I was transferred to a prison that was notorious for its violence. Everyone knew about this place and prayed they wouldn't end up there. Unfortunately, everyone on the prison bus with me was headed to the same facility. This prison was known as the third worst in Tennessee for stabbings, overdoses, rapes, and beatings, ranking thirteenth in the world.

As we arrived, I saw a correctional officer standing at the gate with a shotgun, making it clear that this place was far scarier than where I had been before. While we were registering into the system, an inmate approached us and warned, "As soon as you step on campus, buy a shank." A shank, I learned, is a makeshift knife fashioned from everyday items found in prison, like toothbrushes, razors, and metal from desks. We were in the lion's den, and the first thought that crossed my mind was, "Why here, God? Out of all the prisons in Tennessee, why did you put me here?" The answer would come later.

After we received our belongings, the guards led us to our new living quarters. It became clear how dire our situation was when I saw that my cell had no desk or chair to sit and write on. When I asked some inmates about the missing furniture, they explained that it had been removed to prevent the creation of weapons. I shook my head in disbelief.

When I finally got a chance to use the phone, I called my mom, who had just undergone knee surgery. When she heard where I was, she could only ask, "Why?" I reassured her that we needed to stay strong, trust God, and have faith. I quoted scripture to her, and she did the same for me.

I spent three weeks in that unit before being moved again, this time to one of the worst units on the compound, notorious for stabbings and overdoses. I'm not exaggerating when I say it was chaotic. Before I could even unpack, I heard a commotion. My cellmate welcomed me to

"BA," and as I looked out, I saw a bloody inmate staggering with a prison-made knife sticking out of his head, desperately seeking help. Within minutes, guards and nurses ordered a lockdown. Everyone complied, but shortly after, the doors began popping open again. Incredibly, less than an hour after being stabbed, the injured inmate was returned to the same cell with the same guy who had attacked him. It became clear that these people cared little for human life. My cellmate asked another inmate to pass a string through the door one day. When the inmate did, my cellmate pulled the string back, and the door popped open just like that. Every inmate in that unit rushed out, disregarding the lockdown, and no guard intervened. What shocked me further was the allowance for inmates from different units to visit each other. If someone owed money or goods to an inmate in another unit, guards permitted visits to settle debts, often leading to violent confrontations if the debt wasn't paid. We were only allowed in our cells during headcounts, and we quickly popped out again.

Being out of my cell meant I always had to be on guard, especially during showers. "Shower security" was a term for gang members who would shout it out when their own needed to shower. If you got in their way, you could be charged a fee or face beatings or stabbings for what they perceived as disrespect.

I constantly questioned, "Why did God put me here? Was He testing my faith?" Without a doubt, I believe the answer is yes. God knew how dangerous this place was and how easy it could be to sin. It reminded me of God testing Abraham's faith by asking him to sacrifice Isaac. Even in such a challenging environment, I remained committed to being the person God intended me to be. It was tough, but I kept my distance from trouble, stayed in my Bible, and engaged in Bible studies. I learned the importance of being cautious about who I associated with, as many labeled as believers were false teachers. Surround yourself with those who inspire you to be your best self, but *constantly be discerning; not everyone who claims to be a believer is true to their word.*

Chapter 13

37

In 2021, my now ex-wife served me divorce papers, and I was moved to a different unit in the same prison. This new place was supposed to be better, less strict, and more open. It was an open bay unit, meaning there were no locked doors to keep us confined. We had individual showers with locks and porcelain toilets instead of the usual steel ones.

However, despite these improvements, it was one of the most dangerous units because anyone could access it anytime if they wanted to. This was where I would stay for the next two years.

I attended church every Sunday, continued my theology studies, and participated in a group called Men of Valor, where we held nightly prayer meetings. Despite my efforts, the reality around me was harsh; the devil was always at work. Guards rushed into our unit nearly every day to save lives from overdoses or brutal stabbings. The frequency of these incidents desensitized me to the smell of blood and bleach. It became common to see someone turning blue from a fentanyl overdose and to hear men screaming because they were being assaulted.

I turned to the few people I could call for comfort and hope during these challenging times. My dad was one of them, but my mom was my primary source of support. Outside my family, only one person consistently answered my calls to pray with me, remind me of God's presence, and inspire me to keep walking my path. He was the only man in the church who did this, and I was blessed to call him a friend and brother in Christ.

On January 1, I called to wish my dad a happy seventy-second birthday, unaware of how ill he had become because he didn't want us to worry. Something felt off in his voice, so I called my mom, who knew everything despite their separation. "Is Dad OK?" I asked. She hesitated, and I could hear her voice crack as she started to cry. "Tony, are you sitting down?" I wasn't, so I quickly sat on the floor. "Your dad is sick and has been for a while. He's been on dialysis for a year now." I remembered my dad as a 6'3", 350-pound man, but my mom said he was down to maybe 150 pounds. "They gave him maybe a month to live."

I prayed fervently, asking God to let me see my dad one more time before he passed. I rallied my friends in the prison to pray with me. But God had other plans, and He called my dad home on May 22, 2021. I called my mom to see if he had made it through; when she answered, she said, "He's gone. He wanted to hear your voice before he passed."

All I could do was ask why. Why hadn't my prayer been answered? Was it my selfishness? I believed so. Even though my dad was suffering, I wanted him to hold on until I could see him again. It felt as if my desire for one last moment with him was more important than the pain he endured. Yet I had to remind myself that God's divine intervention had ended his suffering.

Staying true to my faith through this challenging period required me to believe wholeheartedly, even in tough times. I found solace in 1 Peter 1:7 (NLT): "These trials will show your faith is genuine. It is being tested as fire tests and purifies gold—though your faith is far more precious than mere gold. So, when your faith remains strong through many trials, it will bring you much praise, glory, and honor on the day Jesus Christ is revealed to the whole world."

Even though it was hard, I stood firm. I could no longer call my dad and hear him say, "Hey, old man," or "Hey, fathead." I wasn't able to attend his funeral, which hurt deeply. However, perhaps it was a blessing in disguise because I still remembered him as healthy. My mom sent pictures, but they were never the same as seeing him in life. Despite the reality of not seeing him again when I got out, I remained determined to hold onto hope and find new ways to stay connected with him. My mom and I reminisced about our memories together—both good and bad. Some days, we laughed; other days, we cried. I called my friend whenever I could, and he made it a priority to answer, no matter what. He always took the time to connect, whether it was a quick "hi" or a more extended chat. We would discuss the Dallas Cowboys, my life, and our faith, and he would always pray for me and my family before we hung up. Each conversation left me feeling refreshed and inspired. It was a blessing to have someone who cared and didn't judge—a true man of God.

Chapter 14

41

On March 22, 2022, I overcame what once seemed like an insurmountable obstacle. Through unwavering faith and unparalleled determination, I emerged victorious from the worst prison in Tennessee. Despite facing numerous challenges, I refused to falter, and my perseverance paid off. I earned the respect of my fellow inmates by being true to myself and never pretending to be someone I wasn't. Throughout my ordeal, God protected me and answered my prayers, all because of my unshakable faith.

Ephesians 6:10-18, which speaks of the Whole Armor of God, became my guiding principle during my time in prison. I donned that armor daily and stood firm against the devil's schemes. I faced many obstacles but remained steadfast, knowing I was fighting against the spiritual forces of evil. I prayed daily, and my mother—my constant source of strength—prayed for me every morning before heading to work. When I finally walked out of those prison gates as a free man, it felt like a prayer answered. I reunited with my mother, who had patiently awaited my return. I also had the chance to see my children again, some of whom I hadn't seen in years. Witnessing their growth was a surreal experience, but it also highlighted the time I had lost with them. Despite that, I was determined to make things right and be the father they deserved.

Through this journey, I learned that God never abandons us, no matter how challenging our circumstances. I put my faith in Him, trusting He has a plan for my life. I refused to give up and committed to working hard to become the best version of myself. Remarkably, I found a new job just two weeks after my release, thanks to the kindness of a father figure who believed in me and offered me an opportunity I never thought possible. Their support inspired me and brought joy and comfort to my mother during a tough time. Their presence was a true blessing, making every moment count, both good and bad.

On that Sunday, I returned to the church I had attended before, but this time, it was much more extensive and filled with many new faces.

Initially, it was a culture shock. I felt uncertain about who at the church knew me and my past. Although many familiar faces were absent, the paranoia lingered. However, the man who had always answered my calls without judgment welcomed me with open arms. I hugged him tightly and expressed gratitude for his impact on my life in prison. He knew how to alleviate fear, even when it was constantly present.

Thank you for being a guiding light in my darkest hours.

Chapter 15

Five months after my release, I met a woman who would change my life forever. Believe it or not, it all began on social media. Initially skeptical about the potential of our connection, I wasn't entirely honest during our first week of conversations, thinking it wouldn't go far. I expected it to be just a simple "hi," but our communication continued to grow.

Then came the day when she asked a friend to look me up, and the dreaded conversation about my past arose. After we talked, I automatically suggested she might want to leave, as I was used to people exiting my life once they learned about my situation. To my surprise, she expressed that while leaving was a consideration, something kept pulling her toward giving me a chance. And she did. She allowed me to show her that my past did not define me, and I seized that opportunity.

What I thought was impossible, God made possible. I had long believed I would be alone for the rest of my life, thinking, "Who would want to be with someone with a sex offense charge?" But she was willing to take a chance on me. She would be the first person to get me on a plane for our first face-to-face meeting. Nervousness washed over me, and my mother begged me not to go. Yet, despite the doubts and uncertainties, I found the courage to leap into faith and pursue love. It wasn't easy, but I knew she was God-sent when I met someone who accepted me without judgment. So, I took a chance and boarded my first flight to Florida to be with her, all thanks to the power of love and God's guidance.

Although we had initially agreed to avoid a long-distance relationship, the power of love can lead us to make bold decisions. Despite the miles between us, I was determined to make it work because our love was worth it. We planned to repeat our visits in February, but after that, I would be gone from March until June, and I lost my job. She promised to stand by my side, but my past experiences made me skeptical. On June 28, she waited for my call, again proving me wrong.

My mother's unwavering trust, belief, and love toward this woman I met online were genuinely inspiring. Despite her doubts, my mother remained steadfast in her support, reminding me of the power of faith in ourselves and others. Seeing me happy brought her immense joy. In July, my girlfriend flew to Tennessee for the first time, ready to meet her future mother-in-law. When she arrived, we all gathered at a local hibachi grill. Watching them hug each other as if they'd known each other forever was surreal. Witnessing my mother's happiness with the woman I dated was a blessing. Their bond grew strong—a friendship that surpassed all others. She also met the man who had significantly impacted my life, finally understanding why I constantly mentioned him.

After my girlfriend returned home, I faced a frustrating job search that lasted three months. Every time I turned around, it felt like I was searching for something out of reach. Watching my mother struggle daily to make ends meet was heartbreaking, especially knowing I couldn't help. Memories of our past came flooding back, but I was old enough to act this time—yet my background held me back.

As usual, I contacted my go-to person for inspiration and guidance. His prayers have always been a guiding light for me. I shared how close I was to giving up, and he encouraged me to stay on track. After prayer, he reminded me that I could keep moving forward.

Without a license, I rode my bicycle everywhere. One day, while getting some fresh air and talking to God, I passed a temp service with a "Now Hiring" sign. I turned around and headed home, immediately contacting the agency to inquire about job opportunities. Fortunately, they were hiring then and informed me that the employer didn't require background checks. I hurried to the temp agency and filled out the necessary paperwork, and they promised to call me for an interview in a few days.

The following Monday, I attended the interview, enjoyed the walkthrough, and was told to return Tuesday morning to start work. I couldn't wait to call my mother and share the good news. Hearing the relief in her voice as I told her was a release for both of us. I was thrilled about the job and satisfied with the pay, knowing I could finally help my mother without living paycheck to paycheck. Excitedly, I called my girlfriend to tell her God had answered my mentor's prayers. She was relieved and ecstatic. For the first time in a long while, it felt like things were finally looking up for all of us. Yet, despite this progress, I felt that expressing gratitude to God was insufficient.

Chapter 16

October 10, 2023, would be the day when I questioned my faith in God. My once unshakable belief had been shaken, and doubts began to surface. That morning, I had to be at work by 7 a.m. It seemed like a typical day; nothing felt out of the ordinary. My only concern was my mother's complaint about pain in her shoulder blade. We brushed it off, assuming she had just slept wrong, and she took something for relief before dropping me off at work.

At 9 a.m., I received a call from an unknown number. Despite not recognizing it, I answered, needing to know what was happening.

"Antonio?" a voice said.

"Yes, sir?" I replied, anxiety creeping in.

"This is a Wilson County emergency. We need you to go to the hospital as soon as possible. Your mom needs you right now. Please act and go to the hospital immediately—an emergency."

She had just gone to work, and all I could do was call the person she always referred to as her "Person." When she answered, she asked if I had heard what had happened. I told her no, that I had just been told to go to the hospital.

What came next would change my life forever. She told me my mother had passed away due to a massive heart attack. I fell to my knees, crying out, "Why? Why is this happening? I just saw you! I made it clear that I love you. I expected to see you tonight, not this!"

Why hadn't we received a warning? What did I do wrong to deserve this? Those questions echoed in my mind. I fervently hoped that what I heard was a rumor, anxiously waiting for a call to bring good news about her condition.

I declined any offer for a ride, opting to wait for a close friend or family member to arrive. When he arrived, I greeted him with a firm demeanor and asked if she was okay. He shook his head in a 'no' motion. Gasping for air and sobbing uncontrollably, I pleaded for answers. With no answers in sight, I knew I had no choice but to go to the hospital.

Upon arrival, I saw my mother's close friend and brother waiting for me. They immediately grasped my shoulders, knowing I was not well. Then came the most dreadful question from my brother: "Are you ready to see her?" My initial response was a firm "No!" They allowed me a few minutes to gather my thoughts.

Eventually, my brother accompanied me to see our mother lying on the hospital bed. She looked so peaceful, but that was not where she belonged. She was supposed to be my closest companion, protector, and defender with us—the woman I thought would always be by our side. Now what? How do I keep going? Where do I go from here? I was lost and more than broken. I wanted to give up; honestly, I didn't want to be here anymore. What was the point of living? These thoughts plagued me as I struggled with my faith, shaking my fist at God.

As I laid my head on her chest, running my fingers through her hair and wiping the blood from her mouth, I heard her voice in my heart: "Son, you've come too far to let go and give up. God wants you to finish your story."

This brings me to two scriptures that resonate with me:

1. *1 Corinthians 9:24: "Do you not know that in a race all the runners run, but only one receives the prize? So run that you may obtain it."*
2. *2 Chronicles 15:7: "But as for you, be strong and do not give up, for your work will be rewarded."*

Life consists of big and small challenges; we all face them simultaneously. But one thing is for sure: life does not discriminate. You will encounter trials and tribulations no matter who you are or where you come from. The key is to stay strong and positive and never give up. Every obstacle is an opportunity to learn, grow, and improve yourself. So don't be afraid to face life head-on, and keep pushing forward.

Closing Thoughts

As I conclude this journey through the lessons I've learned, I am reminded that life is a continuous discovery process. What I thought I knew has been shaped by experiences, challenges, and the wisdom gleaned from moments of doubt and despair. While often fraught with uncertainty, I understand that our paths lead us to profound insights about ourselves and the world around us.

Every hardship has become a stepping stone toward greater understanding and resilience. I hope my story resonates with you, offering solace and strength in the face of your struggles. Remember, we are not defined by our past mistakes or the labels others place upon us. Instead, we are shaped by our choices, our ability to rise after falling, and our unwavering faith in what lies ahead.

As we navigate life's complexities, let us embrace the lessons that come our way—joyful and painful. May we find beauty in the journey, cherish our moments, and never lose sight of the light that guides us through the darkest days.

Thank you for allowing me to share my experiences with you. I pray that my words inspire you to reflect, grow, and ultimately embrace the profound truth that the grass isn't always greener on the other side, but with faith and perseverance, we can cultivate a garden of hope in our lives.

Acknowledgments

I want to extend my deepest gratitude to a few remarkable individuals who have been a source of unwavering support throughout this journey.

To Scott Marlow, thank you for your constant encouragement and belief in my vision. Your guidance and friendship have been invaluable, and I am truly grateful for your steadfast presence.

To my son, Shawn Banks, you are my pride and joy. Your love, strength, and resilience inspire me every day. I hope this work will serve as a testament to the legacy I wish to leave for you and our family.

To Caroline Inzirillo, thank you for your kindness, insight, and the light you bring into my life. Your support has made all the difference, and I am blessed to have you by my side.

This project would not have been possible without each of you. Thank you from the bottom of my heart.

Did you love *What I Thought I Knew and What I Know Now*? Then you should read *Labeled By Man Chosen By God*[1] by Antonio Banks!

[2]

This book explores how the world sees and labels us, but our labels are transformed when we become new in Christ. In Christ, we are given a new identity that supersedes the labels imposed by society.

Read more at https://antonio-banks.ck.page/ d3e3da6d72?fbclid=IwY2xjawFj3NdleHRuA2FlbQIxMQABHWuK8F5

---

1. https://books2read.com/u/mlz65A

2. https://books2read.com/u/mlz65A

Also by Antonio Banks

Labeled By Man Chosen By God
What I Thought I Knew and What I Know Now

Watch for more at https://antonio-banks.ck.page/
d3e3da6d72?fbclid=IwY2xjawFj3NdleHRuA2FlbQIxMQABHWuK8F5SyfM

About the Author

As an author, I hope my writing will resonate beyond the page, reaching hearts meaningfully. I'm not just telling stories; I'm sharing pieces of myself—my lessons, struggles, and triumphs—with the hope that someone out there will find comfort, strength, and inspiration.

I pray that these pages remind you that you are not alone in your journey and that there is always hope even in moments of uncertainty. Not only that, but I've learned that life isn't about perfection but about perseverance and the beauty of getting back up after a fall. If my words can inspire even one person to keep going, to chase their dreams, or to believe in their resilience, then every late night and every ounce of effort has been worth it.

To anyone reading this, know that your story matters. You can inspire others through words, actions, or quiet acts of courage. Never underestimate the impact you can have. I pray that my books serve as a reminder of that truth, a spark of encouragement that helps light your path forward.

Read more at https://antonio-banks.ck.page/ d3e3da6d72?fbclid=IwY2xjawFj3NdleHRuA2FlbQIxMQABHWuK8F